ARENA

Arena

FIRST EDITION

Printed in the United States of America
ISBN 978-1-880834-72-5

DESIGN ≈ SEVY PEREZ
Adobe Caslon Pro & Fixture

This book is published by the

Cleveland State University Poetry Center
csupoetrycenter.com
2121 Euclid Avenue, Cleveland, Ohio 44115-2214

and is distributed by

SPD / Small Press Distribution, Inc.
spdbooks.org
1341 Seventh Street Berkeley, California 94710-1409

A CATALOG RECORD FOR THIS TITLE IS
AVAILABLE FROM THE LIBRARY OF CONGRESS

ARENA

LAUREN SHAPIRO

For Kevin

I had a dream, which was not all a dream.

—Lord Byron

Presentation 11

Cenotaph 15
The Bodies 16
The Wound 17
Arena 18
Statue 20
Wedge 21
Transition 22
Next to the Arena 24
White Is the New White 26
Feast 27
This and That 28
Cleanse 29
10,000 Dads 30
Projection 31
Arena 32
That Year 34
I Am Your Mother 35
Since Everything Moves at the Atomic Level 36
That One 37
Don't Go There 38
Would You Like to Learn More About Yourself or Others 39
When 42

Lake Space 45

Twinfold 53
Incorporeal 54
Silver Hill 56
The Memory 57
Unspoken Bond 58
The Workshop 59
Arena 60
Thinking About My Father's Suicide Attempts 62
A Baby and His Mother Are One 63
Nothing 64
Ocean Tree 65
Q + A 66
Patience, Patient 67
Spring 68
Imaginary Conversation 70
In Context 71
Aubade 72
Supreme Court Rules Against Women's Contraception Coverage 73
The Arena Empties 74
There Will Be No Memorials 76
Negative Transfer 77
The Kiss 79

Acknowledgements 83

PRESENTATION

First I will say what I am going to say about loss and then I will say it. Later I will repeat what I said so that you will remember the important points when you are doing something else like watering the garden or picking up your kid from school. Probably if you have experienced a deep loss you will already know what I am going to say. If so, feel free to chime in. I will stick to the facts and will avoid any figurative language. My references will include only the most recent and cutting-edge research. This will not be a self-help session but rather a tool to better understand the psychological intricacies of your own particular emotional trauma. This is about you but also about all of humanity over time. Because everyone is different, please don't quote me. I will be as sensitive as possible while remaining true to the professional approach. My examples will be real but will not include my own experiences. Before their deaths, I will refer to the people as Mr. X and Ms. Y. After their deaths, I will refer to them as Body X and Body Y. This should clear up any confusion over the timeline of events or the physical or emotional presences of these people.

[redacted]

CENOTAPH

There is a reliquary on a ledge outside the bathroom.

No one really knows why. I mean, that was the winter my father tried to kill himself.

I was getting a haircut when I received the call. Then I kept receiving it forever.

I was talking about the Christmas preparations at the time. Debating the kinds of lights to get or something.

It must have been a muddy time, said someone. Actually, it was terrifying.

Later the doctor told us it was impossible to tell what anything meant, though he didn't use those words.

Someone used the metaphor of the iceberg. You know, what's showing and what's not. Someone else mentioned black holes. None of it made sense but I guess they were nice gestures?

I mean, at least they were trying?

Someone still had to buy groceries and shovel the snow and all that.

Then my father cashed out the savings account and gave us each a check.

I kept trying to piece together events as though the questions could be answered logically. Then I realized I had all the wrong questions.

Someone strung yellow tape to the driver's side door of the car.
No one knew who had brought flowers.

Some actions are more meaningful. Like leaving a note.

Then I remembered the baby.

Oh no, where was the baby?

THE BODIES

The bodies on the battlefield
in the documentary aren't really
dead of course they position
themselves for sunrise I'm told
the bodies get $25 and free lunch
the bodies are trying to make it
in Hollywood or just anywhere
being a lawyer or a sanitation worker
the bodies might be feeling exhausted
or just done with it all before
I was born the body put a bag
over its head and disappeared
I was six when the body forever
jumped from a bridge thirty when
the body tried again and again
to fly from the top of the parking
garage the bodies make a pattern
of loss they can't see or stop
after the movie shoot the bodies
pick themselves up and wash off
their wounds the bodies take
a sandwich then it's the easiest thing
the bodies just get in their cars
and drive home

THE WOUND

And when the flower opens its wound?
And when the wound is mortal, fanned out
like makeup spilled from a purse?
And it's always your one and only wound,
the one you keep coming back to?
And the purse was stolen from an old lady
who died before it could be returned?
And there was absolutely nothing of interest
in the purse anyway?
And the purse was a symbol, as was the empty bus
and the cat carcass in the gutter and everything else
you saw that day?
And in every other way the day was normal?
And the famous scholar made many statements of truth
that couldn't touch you?
And you longed for the days you were so easily touched?
And went home and became even more obsessed
with the wound until everything in the house was related
to the wound and your destiny was the wound
was being with it forever and forever
letting it consume you completely your body
shedding itself like so much of nothing
and the wound opening into something
else entirely some part of your mind that
had always essentially known it as home?

ARENA

To imagine your world encircled is to imagine it
finite, a spectacle   The best place for a goring
is the center of the storm   where everything
is still, like a microscope the doctors pore over,
probing   When the crowd quiets it's to
see the decapitation or just to breathe in,   *not me*
How insular, I mean lucky,   to be sitting
in the arena, to be outside   the center   The show
must go on and on   If you close your eyes it
goes on   Later you could mention what you
hear   how the only reason you know it's over
is the sudden and incredibly loud   cheers

STATUE

She was a cathedral
She was up every morning
She inspired awe and scorn variously
She was greater than the sum of her parts
After a while she had no more parts to speak of
She was forever crumbling
She was from the Roman Empire
before there were cathedrals
She was an aqueduct
that carried rainwater to the mouths of children and animals
She was without conscious thought
She didn't understand her purpose
She didn't know she even had one

WEDGE

I find the old bills
the ones printed on pink, *final notice*
Living in a beautiful house we couldn't afford
with even a pool and a giant yard that required a riding mower
and living there as though we belonged
When you and Mom visited, willing the baby to smile at you,
willing him to crawl good-naturedly over your leg,
to really enjoy the toy you brought, to ham it up in a baby way
I silently begged him to do something just *do something*
but he was cranky as usual
he climbed out of your lap when I put him in
he threw a full-on tantrum
while you looked vacantly at the wall
when I offered lasagna Mom said *I hate lasagna*
when I offered a glass of wine you had to drive
I had to hold it together
what did any of it mean
now we lived in a cul-de-sac with all kinds of baby stuff
I couldn't talk to anyone
You didn't say a word
Then you spoke mechanically, the machine gears grinding in your brain
You pulled out your wallet
and handed me a check

TRANSITION

When my father went missing
a second time my brother
drove to the top of the vacant

parking garage, expecting
demolition, maybe loose
beams, December birds—

but there was a white car.
A single stone dropped
in his lungs. Running?

I imagine him running
to the rail where my father
clung, my brother grabbing

him in a bear hug and screaming
to the police who had gathered
below, unnecessary screws

in the punctured moment that
continued its expansion inward
at the pace of adrenaline, a second

existence opening, a different life,
two entirely different people.
But my father didn't want saving,

he began to unzip his coat.
Just let go and I'll come back
over the rail, he said to my

brother. That would be
a kind of ending, if you
wanted it. But everything

became cloudy after the police
put my father in the patrol car
and left my brother standing

there, blown into loss like living
nothing, breathing as if his body
were just his body.

NEXT TO THE ARENA

there is a beach that is always full   of people
doing brightly colored   watersports there are
inflatable unicorns   the smell of sunscreen and
cigarettes   I'm told it's always sunny you can
rent a parasol   or buy ice cream and hotdogs
for cheap   there's no reason not to go   if you're
in town but know on days   the arena is open
you might hear cheers   or screams you might
smell something resembling   charred meat

WHITE IS THE NEW WHITE

Bleak the new bleak
Sun the only sun you'll ever see
Repetition the brother of invention
Invention a small hole in a star
so far away no one believes it's there
That's okay, your invention is private
It's not groundbreaking or patentable
It can't be squeezed into juice
or sold on the corner
Your invention must be viewed with special sunglasses
that can be found in a field
an hour outside of town
You should know there is also a mass grave in this field
You have to step around the many scattered bones
but it's okay
even a kid could do it

FEAST

My mother puts the platter in front of me
and without thinking I take a bite
It's Christmas after all and we're at the end
of a holiday movie
When I used to imagine your death
it was so cliché
I would picture your absence
like an underground tunnel
taking me into a lonely woodland clearing
where a single bird chirped her red song
but now I imagine your body
floating in the Quinnipiac River
with your wallet in a Ziploc duct-taped to your arm
now you are sprawled in an impossible star
by the pay station of the tallest parking garage
and some idiot finds you first
you are dredged from the bottom of the icy lake
where we used to take the dog each Sunday
there are so many ways
to be angry   I mean
lonely   when I open
the glass box on Christmas
it's just air inside   I mean
it's all air inside   the box is bursting
you have to think hard
to see anything at all
to see   the air I mean

THIS AND THAT

This is a sunburn
and that is a night shadow over a puddle,
this the long-awaited moment of impact with the ground
and that my feelings hiding behind a shroud of sand,
this is the endless anticipation of that, metamorphosing
into a nightmare in space,
this right here is what I've been trying to tell you,
that there is little difference between is, was, and had been
except insofar as we understand the meaning of time,
this snowball about to incinerate itself
just by existing in that kind of heat,
this life about to be shuttled into the distant past
by that sudden, irrevocable event,
this father about to become
that father about to become
just this other one

CLEANSE

There's something in the water in the hand cream the over-the-counter vitamins the FDA has not required labeling doesn't understand the toxic microbes in the genetically engineered tomatoes in the plastic that your food comes wrapped in the ink on the packaging the gum on the sticker on the apple the unclean facilities where the spinach is chopped and bagged the lowering standards of organic yogurt it's in the plastic on the baby mattress and the bottles and sippy cups the fabric your kids' clothes are made of if you shop at Target forget about it unless you buy local organic small farm handmade in the U.S.A. if you even consider buying any kind of meat or dairy if you have your own garden be careful of chemical runoff bird shit can cause salmonella a raw diet will cleanse the bowels but may contain toxins unless cooked to 150 degrees at which point nutrients are lost try to find natural supplements and antioxidants you may harvest wild berries that have not been touched by bears or deer which carry bacteria on their tongues remember not to rinse in tap water or allow to touch plastic of any kind if it sits too long it is susceptible to airborne bacteria but the bacteria in the refrigerator is worse ideally eat the food flash-cooked immediately after it has been picked if you are sure your hands are clean.

10,000 DADS

We have 10,000 dads. *You're so lucky!* say all our friends. *You're so complicated!* say all our therapists. *Your mom must be so hot!* say all the sleazebags. But sometimes it's hard. Having 10,000 homes and 10,000 toothbrushes is tricky. The holidays are rough, and remembering every dad's birthday is impossible. Saying good morning takes all day. Life is a constant fight for attention. They beg and plead with us to have a meal with them or hit around some baseballs. They follow us religiously on Instagram and like all our posts. They have such good hearts, the 10,000 dads. But how well do we really know any of them?

PROJECTION

Ten tons of loss are couched within the beaming old lady.
Where you see them is not where things are.
Where you go looking is not where they are.
Read Heidegger, he'll tell you better than I could,
if you can get through the bric-a-brac.
The rain turns to snow then back to rain.
I project truth and honor and pity onto the weather.
The earth begins its apology.
I put a magnifying glass to my husband's sleep mumbling.
People have been doing this forever.
Another student begins *Since the dawn of mankind,*
which is another way of saying *I don't know where to start.*
The wedding gushes like a waterfall of brackish water.
When I was young, I would vomit all the time,
but now my body stores anxiety deep in its bedrock.
As I run the dishwasher and take out the recycling,
I can hear a distant bird chanting its sad song.

ARENA

It's encouraged to bring a knife or   a sling shot
a man fills a water gun   with acid a nerf gun
with poisoned darts   the sign says it's healthy
to let off steam   there is a lot of anger in the arena
the police stand idly by   this seems like a violent
rerun   but the news says it's real people tune in
to the story then go back   to their desk jobs
if you're in the arena   look it's easy to see
the body puddled   in the center but which of all
of those which one   was the murder weapon

THAT YEAR

I sent postcards of water to my family members.
Come visit! I shouted from my spot on the beach.
The water came in and out like a lung, and the sun
kept pocketing itself in protest. Exploring
the strange depths of despair, I found
a horse, a compact, and a nurse named Wilma
who told me I was untreatable. Go sun yourself,
she said. Enjoy what you have left. I believed
Wilma like I believed the doctor and the TV anchor
and the little boy who thumbed his nose at me
in the science museum. The librarian said,
Please leave through the back door.
My dog wouldn't even come for a treat.
Holding the black rock in my hand, I couldn't tell
where it ended and the rest of the world began.
I was stuck in the candy aisle of Rite Aid forever
only I had no teeth. I'm so tired of hearing about
your dreams, said my husband in my dream.
Come back soon, said the cashier who charged me
a dollar an hour to keep living. I think I lost something,
I told her, and she pretended to be sorry
so I would feel loved as I journeyed to the underworld.
When I got there I saw that I'd been there
all along, only I kept dreaming that I was alive.
Do you have a family? a large silver bird asked me
from his cage of music and rust. I don't know,
I said. I'm confused. The bird looked at me strangely.
I was speaking a different language. I must always have
been speaking this other language no one understood.

I AM YOUR MOTHER

But you took yourself away from me

I hung lights from every part of my body
and mirrors so that you would see
my grief glistening

I was never not looking for you
even before you left
I was looking for you

You couldn't see it
because you were always waiting to be found
Only we lived in different oceans by then

I ate seaweed to survive
You didn't eat anything
There was nothing to drink in the ocean
We might have died of thirst
if you hadn't left for good
and forced me to give up

There are animals
who don't care
about that sort of thing

You left an infinite tunnel
You left a radioactive pile of clothes
Not even the philosophers could help me
make sense of it

For a long time I said you'd been abducted
even though I knew
everyone knew

So I took the single gray pill
you'd left on my nightstand

SINCE EVERYTHING MOVES AT THE ATOMIC LEVEL

and since a loaded gun says something about the loader
by the time the animated body had ceased
and the subpar machinery had been recalled
by the time the manufacturer had claimed responsibility
and the system had tabulated the loss
by the time the production line had been fixed
and since human error is unquantifiable
by the time those involved had been notified
and since we can't know about intention
at that time the police became involved
at that time it ceased to be a family affair

THAT ONE

His eyes are two planes flying through thunder.
His breath a thousand miniature ponies stomping in the morning mist.
His feet are two felled trees before they become paper.
His hair, indescribable.
His demeanor, the smoldering ashes of the fires at the trailer park.
His dogs, the wild ponytails of imagination.
His writing, profound.
His calendar, set to repeat.
Many are the times I have wanted to shatter the side mirrors of his Escalade.
Abundant are the fruits of his disregard.
When I open the window, he turns on the heat.
When I crack the book, he disappears in its pages.
I am at the Rare Book Library and must wear gloves.
I can't afford his lavish orders at Starbucks anymore.
His genius refuses to be classified.
His rage is the rage of privilege.
His arms are the arms of the last word.

DON'T GO THERE

You walk into oncoming traffic.
The pool of blood is black, black, etcetera.
Your brother throws himself from a bridge
onto a playground. He holds a plastic bag
over his head. It is a grocery bag, the same kind
you use on Sundays, etcetera.
Your mind is black like the blood.
You never walked into traffic, but you thought about it.
And jumping from the parking garage, etcetera.
Your body and mind are two trees
in the same yard, casting shadows on each other.
The children have picnics there, and run around, etcetera.
No, that's not right. There were no picnics,
no summer, etcetera. You never stayed in one place.
An ocean couldn't hold you. You disappeared
every morning when you woke up.
I walked in at breakfast and didn't understand.
The waves came in, in, in, etcetera.
The pile of rocks in the yard became a furnace
no one could crawl out of, etcetera.
From my place in the black corner
all I could see was myself. I was a child.
I didn't know anything, not even
etcetera, etcetera, etcetera.

you can assume your identity will be protected how interested are you in discovering your true self is this something you'd be prepared to admit your hoarding I mean has it become a problem in your marriage do you slam it in a drawer when someone walks in the room are you embarrassed do you find it meaningful the old shampoo and toothpaste cartons the stacks of printed emails packages on packages of doublemint gum do you remember the provenance of each item under the bed does it make you feel happy and then very sad is this a way to live is there a trash can in this room will you use all ten magnifying glasses in case you decide to go on a picnic you will need the travel mayonnaise it is possible there will be a use for each piece of wrapping paper there is probably information in the magazine that would interest an acquaintance there is a story behind the bag of plastic bags the many brochures it's a straightforward case they call this a compulsion but how could they possibly know the medical establishment how could they

INK

WHEN

When I stopped taking the medication
When I opened the window and saw
the long shadows on the lawn and saw
myself in the shadows forever
When I had a coffee and popped an antihistamine
and gazed onto the expanse and saw myself as a worm
When I saw myself as less than a worm
As a blade of grass on the artificial lawn
that a happy man had created and enjoyed
cultivating every Saturday
When I stopped taking the medication
When I knew that I could allow
myself to be manufactured
to be happier
When I knew with certainty
When I thought of my family
It made me sad
It made me sad

[redacted]

LAKE SPACE

When the note had been found
When I was running blindly through the marsh
I asked anyone anyone if they had seen your body
walking if they had seen a moving body
that looked like you
somewhere near the water's edge I said
excuse me sir excuse me ma'am I said
by any chance have you seen I said
the December muck from the marsh now through my shoes
and up my leg I said something that felt
a thousand miles from my balloon heart
what I said exactly I can't even
my body felt the futility but said it anyway
my body ran and ran until it couldn't
until there was no one left to ask no one
to see no place for a body that hadn't been
no place at all until my body couldn't catch
its breath felt like it couldn't stop until
my body felt and knew it couldn't

so he was found
so he was committed
so they let him out
you are cured, they said
and sent him out
to where sunlight is an oppressive brick
and the people are mechanized
and happy just beetling around
to where life is a clump of dirt nestled in the bone
of a tree where a dog likes to shit
and each step takes you to the same plateau
and after that plateau there is another
and another just like it
this is the world, they say
this is the start, they say
congratulations, they say

then

How will
you tell
me how
will you
tell me
how tell
will you
tell me how
will you
how will
you were
you even
going to

there was a girl by the lake
she was walking a dog down
their usual path when
they came upon the space

uninhabited, the stranger gone
the dog took a sip of cold
water as his nature asked
in the space where there could
have been a body
a vacuum in the space that
was itself bright and cold
good for the lungs
if you aren't in despair
maybe if you want to
hum or even sing

I wanted a song
more than anything

I wanted a song that comes
full circle with an end that explains
the beginning and a beginning that erupts
out of the deep body

I wanted a chorus to relay the message
again and again, simply, and for
the many crows to provide
the only drama as they leave
the barren tree

I wanted the song to be sung
to the barren tree
and for the silence
of the tree to be meaningful

I wanted the answer to the destruction
of the body by the body, the body that
made me to be found in the tree
and in the song to the tree

more than anything

I wanted a song

[redacted]

TWINFOLD

In blackout times   being vigilant might be
more about the body   you have to descend
from your location   on the osprey perch maybe
you didn't know you   were there though you
helped build it years   ago and watched the machine
install the perch over   the beautiful and sinking
marsh it's easy to feel   sorrow for the mother
of the dead boy   and also for the mother
of the shooter but in   blackout times one must
resist the urge   to humanize those who
commit structural   violence also those who
continue to look away   from the carcasses lining
the street the shadows   of doubt blooming
the urge to say   *they didn't know* or
they were just doing   *their job* the blasted tree
the furnace reminders   a pile of shoes the children
who don't understand   reminders the signs still
perched in triumph on   the manicured lawns
reminders the electronic   diaries of the traumatized
girls reminders   the Internet will feed you
algorithms of yourself   you can like them a thousand
times but you will have   to move your body toward
places it is not used to   going you will have to
practice the new art   of seeing of being angry
at yourself it's okay   to say hello to strangers
to cross the path to   plant aggressively the seeds
that have been bred   to grow in darkness

INCORPOREAL

Smile at the play date   bring snacks
and through the window   watch
the enormous trees   tower over
the mansions   down the expansive
street in the snow   be very far away
from sound,   from bodies in the room
the bodies of your family   be insulated
from any noise or thought   your own
body might make   the committee
of happy living requests your presence
in another universe   it's easy to feel
your way there   all you have to do
is pretend   you're someone else

SILVER HILL

I hadn't thought
it would be a country
club kind of place
he was resistant
to group therapy
the rich kids getting
off coke, my father
seemed not-at-all home
we sat in the sitting
room and said nothing
you could think forever
about an ocean
and never drown
a body might be
furniture after all,
the kind in a formal
room for receiving
guests we ask each
other nothing
questions like what
did you eat today
we imagine how
the weather might
change feels like
we'll be here forever
since no one knows
how to leave

THE MEMORY

is like wool like the toy llama
made from real llama fur
that's the kind of appropriation I feel
when I write about you
it's a secret about a secret
a lie about a lie
you have to open a thousand doors
and enter the endless maze to see it
the photo of the photo of the dog
dying on the porch the candy
inside the candy I would like to extract
a melody from the memory
not unlike a beach inside a beach
there's no water anywhere at this beach
it's actually a desert
you have to use your imagination
I'm sipping a piña colada made of a pinecone
the cars going by make ruinous tracks
in my daydream the noise is consistent
I've seen it on TV on the infomercial
for a bubble that never pops
can we get it can we get it
pleads my son from inside
the poppable bubble
in which we live

UNSPOKEN BOND

He gave me his grandmother's emerald engagement earrings
and said, *Don't tell my mother.*
I gave him my grandfather's ancient Roman coin
and said, *Don't tell my father.*
Then he gave me his father's war medal
and I gave him my mother's Olympic trials trophy
and he gave me his mother's Chanel suit
and I gave him my father's gold cuff links
and then we each stole cash from our parents
and threw it at each other in handfuls like leaves
and greedily picked it all up and laughed
and threw it again, this time with feeling
and we kissed and kissed and kissed and kissed like that forever.

THE WORKSHOP

One student writes an intricate poem using a spider web as metaphor for a failed romantic relationship. Another writes a political manifesto with line breaks. Three write autobiographical narratives about childhood traumas. I am also a student but when I turn in my imagined historical encounter between Clara Barton and Florence Nightingale the other students look at me and say, *Write what you know*. Next week I turn in a poem about a poet who is tired of other poets' lousy personal narratives so she brings in a gun and shoots all the poems in the chest before taking the life of her own poem. The professor calls campus security. At the station, the police officer asks me questions about my family and emotional state. *This isn't about me*, I say. *This is a failure of imagination. We take this kind of thing very seriously*, he says. *It isn't a joke.* His office is full of the usual detritus—framed certificates of completion and honor, the college calendar, an inspirational photo of skydivers. On his desk there is a picture of his wife and two young children. He sees me looking at it and turns it away.

ARENA

A shirt and shoes are required your
signature on the dotted line your fingerprints
license plate the reason you came here in
the first place what you saw in the Arena
whose blood do you know whose blood is all over
the fucking promenade? Did you come here
to see someone die to get a jolt eat cotton candy
and popcorn hear the symphony eulogize
him is that pig's blood was the sacrifice human
was it a spectacle you wanted a show with all
the bells and whistles a Las Vegas in lights were
you expecting Mariah Carey were you waiting
for the signal to applaud was your response
prerecorded we ask that you wear only dark
colors out of respect no low-cut blouses or
short-shorts and try not to be the idiot
who brings a boom box or drone who posts
to Instagram remember that this
festival is also a funeral

THINKING ABOUT MY FATHER'S SUICIDE ATTEMPTS

To block the thoughts I try
unsticking the butter
from itself, baking muffins,
the many deflated balloons
from my son's party must be
thrown out all the TV I let him
watch is about hero dogs
saving animals trapped in ice
or trees they only have
to return the baby to its mother
they just have to pick up the apples
that spilled in the orchard,
the disasters are simple,
the solution is obvious.
This is how a kid's mind works,
I think, but then sometimes
at night before bed he cries
and when I ask him what's wrong
he says *If I'm really bad*
will you send me to live on
another planet alone
forever? I am shocked at
his capacity to imagine
such a terrible punishment—
No, no, I tell him,
You must stay with me forever,
You must never leave, I say.
But what if, he says,
I do something, he says,
What if I do something
really, really bad?

A BABY AND HIS MOTHER ARE ONE

Some days I killed you
others I let you suffer in a dark corner
I was a cold stone in the corner
and you were the golden bird flying over
with the world's blessings
I amassed the miniature holiday decorations
that sent a paltry glow over your distant belly
I was just a mother and you were the most popular toy
this holiday season
You made a variety of noises when a button was pushed
and came with different moods
By watching you others could learn
to express themselves more eloquently
Once I had an urge to throw you from the window
of a high rise and follow you down
Once I had an urge to sleep forever in the dark woods
of your discontent
but now I run after the harried threads you trail
from your fingers like.fairy dust
I pick up the rosebuds you leave lying in your soiled clothes
We are blossoming into new people
We are aging in a meaningful way

NOTHING

I wondered how long I would be on fire
I wondered would there come a different moment
The myth came carrying its history like grandma's gold teeth
in their little box of time
I was too young, I was frightened
I didn't know about going without
I didn't know about the horseman lowering his sack
and shaking out nothing at all on the ground
I didn't know about nothing
I had never thought about it
how it breathes a wreath of fire
every time you look at it

OCEAN TREE

The empty tree is an archaic key
in the blue morning. No one
had touched me for a year,
but I didn't know it until
a stranger gave me a hug.
I'm used to the humiliations
of familial love. I cried all over
the seagull but it kept coming
back. I knelt at the altar
and recognized a God. My family
had scattered into skeletons
across the world. I forgot the word
for mother. I had never learned
the word for father. I was terrified
of language so I remained silent
at water's edge. I heard a sound
but it was only a vision of my mind
wrapped in cellophane, sweating.
I could hear the pulse of a baby
in motion. I adopted all the pets
but was still alone. I opened my arms
to touch the beautiful butterflies
as they landed like leaves coming back
to a dead tree. I was the tree.
I could only understand the present.
I can only understand the present.

Q + A

Do you have any scars Are you aware that you are wearing two different shoes What was your last meal Do you still believe the CIA is after you Have you considered other uses for shoelaces Have you always avoided holiday parties How often do you lie to those you care about Why did you bring the Ziploc bag When was the last time you felt happy Have you thought recently about ending your life and do you have a plan Why do you think I am asking What will the diagnosis mean if you lie will it be different if there is no diagnosis can you leave is it over yet will there be an end to the questions who wants to know these things who is important in the scenario when will it end the scenario I mean has it played itself out who will be waiting at home will someone be able to pick you up what will you tell them who will give the answer what if there is no answer of course there is an answer it just takes a while you may have to try different medications there will be side effects in trying to find the solution it will be necessary to ask the right questions do you think these are the right questions

PATIENCE, PATIENT

Once I was driving for a long time
by myself, tediously, as people do
when they have to get between two
distant points in a country that thinks
it is not at war and I was listening
to a radio show about how little
compassion Americans seem to have,
how silent and insular they become
before erupting in a firework of bullets.
President Obama said *I don't think we have*
a monopoly on crazy people. The woman said
she was trying to make a point by banging
the loaded shotgun on the floor before
blowing off her jaw. Of course we must
think about the deer population and terrorists
in the wilderness next door as well as
the stupidity of most people trying to make
a point about rights, etcetera. Then the show
ended and some classical music came on
which reminded me how long some things
can endure, for example a sonata written
before radio or this country really existed,
how we still find it beautiful. I considered
how I could have this thought alone
in Ohio, the blank highway a pointless
connection between two extremes.
Then I paid the toll and drove on.

SPRING

The nice teachers at the kindergarten open house
point out the Unifix cubes and color game;
they are professional in their analysis of play.
At Lainy's party the operators of Jump 'N Bounce
look away while kids wrestle into their idyllic
selves. A mother tells me, hushed, how
one November morning Jason's father parked the car
and blew his head off. Then it's time for cake.
The kids are sweaty, tumbling over each other
for a spot at the table. I search Jason's face
for a sign, a scar, but don't find it—he's blowing
a noisemaker in Sean's face, his mother chatting
pleasantly in the corner. Cue the birthday music.
Next day, we're late, and I walk my distressed son
into school. *We're gonna miss the eggs hatching!* he yells,
bounding down the stairs. The class is huddled
around the incubator, the glow from the heat lamp
flushing their faces. This must be a rite of passage,
watching a chick's birth surrounded by friends.
It's on the docket, tailored to the lesson plan, deemed
developmentally appropriate. It's March, after all,
when the world glosses over its losses.

IMAGINARY CONVERSATION

He said it felt like getting dead very
slowly if you could imagine it
Maybe, I said, *like people caught*
in a flood watching the waters rise
No, he said, *more like a constant tripping*
toward pavement, watching it speed
up, that panicky feeling all the time
As we talked his scars prickled out like
constellations of mourning in reverse
and I could see all of his family
I could hear them as though they were a wild herd
of family bellowing at their stray and
the conversation started to feel like
a funnel sucking me into a strange outback
populated by dead grass and shadows where
no one thought of food or missed the sun
or each other where even the animalistic
moment passed unheeded and darkness
became one with the body a long glove
where darkness made the mind switch
off where the body was caught in
a long glove the body didn't notice

IN CONTEXT

The people in the coffee shop talk about boutique
firms and methodology while behind them strange
artwork morphs out of the wall in 3-D. The mother
and her five-year-old have an argument about clothes
in front of the pregnant nude photographs she had
commissioned in her third trimester, when the world
felt heavy but easy and she used websites like Pinterest
without irony. I read the tabloids alongside the news headlines
and the interest pieces on Buzzfeed like "Woman with Third Boob
Wants to Be Unattractive to Men." Meanwhile my students
are writing terrible and heartbreaking poems about children
dying in Syria and we discuss the necessity of imagery
and *show, don't tell.* At this point I am a robot regurgitating
tropes and when I tell my students we are going on a field trip
one smartass says she hopes it's not to the art museum *again*,
and I say no, not to worry, we're going to a sweatshop up the street,
and I sense some of my students are scared and some are excited
and they are all clutching their notebooks and pencils
as we line up outside the building, which is made of dark concrete
with no windows and which seems to be vibrating slightly
the way all my students are vibrating slightly
and everyone stands on tiptoe and peers around each other
as I slowly open the door.

AUBADE

Seasonally, the world says what to do:
Prepare, stay warm, loosen, run.
The party balloon shrinks and shrinks
until it's just a prune in the corner.
Driving the long way through the park
to get to the doctor's office where
the kids fight over the videogame.
I won't allow myself to become
is a phrase that often appears on listservs—
also *sending light*. Are you sure
that's a good idea? says the man
to the pregnant woman in the coffee shop.
Explain the difference between smog
and fog to a child. Make the damn brownies
you've been promising for weeks. Also,
resist the urge to universalize your life,
the kids walking around all day in metaphors.
Truly, this is just about taking out the trash,
packing a lunch, wiping the shit off his ass.
Then the political comes barging in off the news,
a beacon lighting the institutional miseries
you'd almost forgotten about. The world
splashes in, hangs out in the corner.
The colorful gifts lie silent.
I should have said it was still dark.
Now the black sky begins to purple
around the trees as the street lights
click off in unison.

SUPREME COURT RULES AGAINST WOMEN'S CONTRACEPTION COVERAGE

Is that a shark?
No, it's a wave.
Is that a lizard?
No, it's a stick.
Is that a dead mermaid floating on a brick of gold?
Yes, that is a dead mermaid floating on a brick of gold.
Better bury her.

THE ARENA EMPTIES

In organized waves   down escalators in hallways
full of bodies moving forward   as one then dispersing
someone bends into a corner and vomits   people
step around   engineers have designed an orderly
evacuation   it takes only fifteen minutes then
workers clear the wrappers and beer   the remains
of fireworks and blood   there's a cleaning solution
for difficult stains   there's a machine that handles
heavy refuse   the process is mechanized
to purge the space   of physical residues to eradicate
unfavorable smells   to get it ready for tomorrow

PNC BANK

THERE WILL BE NO MEMORIALS

The bust painstakingly carved in the Renaissance manner
is dumped in the Walmart parking lot.

Anger shines its branding iron on the pastel sky.

Cut to a motionless fairy garden, the winged sprites
glued to their grassy stations.

I'm prepared to find the body, but turns out
it's just a row of tulips.

Who makes a fairy garden, anyway?
There's an aisle at Michael's with tiny bridges, wells, moss-covered rocks, bells.
You could spend a fortune on a microcosm.

Who goes to Michael's, anyway?
A stick of incense, a wave of high-school memories sloughing off like dead skin.

You call to work out the logistics: flight times, tax information.
I'm fine, you say. *Work's good. Expecting snow.*

It's like this never happened. Did it happen?

I stock up on beads and kids craft items. The sun comes in slant, preparing itself
for another season.

I want you to bring it up. I want you to say you've been thinking about it, too.

Spring arrives with all its distant babies.

We creep closer to our separate homes.

NEGATIVE TRANSFER

If I admire the catastrophe
would it cease to be a catastrophe?
They say crystals open up new
avenues of thought when paired
with dim lighting and a certain
kind of spa music. In other words,
to forgive someone, spend some
time in a steam room. You know,
I can mail you a puddle any time—
you just have to destroy
the packaging. But also, why
would you want a puddle?
And why would you want to
hold a mirror to your mind's
distant, angry pumping? At night
I read the beautiful poetry about
insomnia written by the insomniac
poet and think, everything refers
back to itself. I try meditation
and imagine my father rising
out of a majestic purple flower,
turning into an angel. When
I open my eyes, all I see is
a dinky plastic waterfall. To resist
metaphor you must have an iron
will. When the neighbor mows
his lawn in his shorty pajamas
at five a.m., he's just mowing
his lawn. The animals and
shrubbery are just being
animals and shrubbery. I watch
the student competing with himself

for most productive self. I watch
the pets in the pet store, lined up
like beers. Is it possible not to have
a meltdown? Did I mention I've
tried meditation? When I was
finished, I had tearfully forgiven
my father. Then I drank some
lemon water and ate some healthy
spa snacks. In art, the first thing
you learn is the importance
of negative space. In philosophy
it's the distinction between
negative space and nothing.
The spa lady smiles and hands me
a water bottle for the road. Real
forgiveness is like a puddle's
slow and muddy evaporation.
If I keep picking bits of thread
from the sweater, eventually
the whole thing will disappear.

THE KISS

I would like to kiss you, said the man
perched on the chimney, *but I don't have*
any lips. From my spot on the roof
I told him I was married but that if
he didn't have lips it would be okay.
He came near and touched me softly
on my cheek with his cheek and I knew
that he really did have lips but was
being kind because he could tell that
I was blind and lonely sitting on a roof
in winter and he wanted to bring me back inside.

ACKNOWLEDGMENTS

I am grateful to the journals in which some of these poems first appeared, sometimes in altered form: *Bennington Review, Boston Review, Columbia Poetry Review, Copper Nickel, Devil's Lake, DIAGRAM, Forklift, Ohio, jubilat, Mississippi Review, New Ohio Review, Pittsburgh City Paper, Propeller,* and *Wave Composition.*

I am grateful to friends and colleagues who looked at this manuscript or simply offered support: Michelle Gil-Montero, Lauren Haldeman, Dan Rosenberg, Jerry Costanzo, Jane McCafferty, Jane Bernstein, Jason England, Heidi Wiren Bartlett, Suzanne Buffam, Darcie Dennigan, and Clare Beams. Thank you also to Carnegie Mellon University, which provided crucial time and additional support in the form of a Falk Research Grant.

I am especially grateful for the vision and editing work of Caryl Pagel, and for the help of all those who work with the Cleveland State University Poetry Center, including Hilary Plum, the talented designer Sevy Perez, and the many graduate students who were involved in this project.

I had my Bubbe, Rita Shapiro, in the back of my mind some moments while writing this book.

I am grateful to my parents, who taught me much even in very difficult times, and to my brother and sister, Dan and Amy, who were there.

My children, Javi and Eliza, have taught me and changed me.

Finally, I am grateful to my husband, Kevin, who was and is by my side.

LAUREN SHAPIRO is the author of *Easy Math* (Sarabande, 2013), which was the winner of the Kathryn A. Morton Prize and the Debut-litzer Prize for Poetry, as well as a chapbook of poems, *Yo-Yo Logic* (DIAGRAM/New Michigan Press, 2011). With Kevin González, she co-edited *The New Census: An Anthology of Contemporary American Poetry* (Rescue Press, 2013). She is an associate professor of English at Carnegie Mellon University.

RECENT CLEVELAND STATE UNIVERSITY POETRY CENTER PUBLICATIONS

Edited by Caryl Pagel & Hilary Plum

POETRY

World'd Too Much: The Selected Poetry of Russell Atkins
ed. Kevin Prufer and Robert E. McDonough
Advantages of Being Evergreen by Oliver Baez Bendorf
My Fault by Leora Fridman
Orient by Nicholas Gulig
Age of Glass by Anna Maria Hong
In One Form to Find Another by Jane Lewty
50 Water Dreams by Siwar Masannat
daughterrarium by Sheila McMullin
The Bees Make Money in the Lion by Lo Kwa Mei-en
Residuum by Martin Rock
Festival by Broc Rossell
Sun Cylce by Anne Lesley Selcer
Bottle the Bottles the Bottles the Bottles by Lee Upton

ESSAYS

I Liked You Better Before I Knew You So Well by James Allen Hall
A Bestiary by Lily Hoang
Codependence by Amy Long
The Leftovers by Shaelyn Smith

TRANSLATIONS

Scorpionic Sun by Mohammed Khaïr-Eddine translated by Conor Bracken
I Burned at the Feast: Selected Poems of Arseny Tarkovsky translated by
Philip Metres and Dimitri Psurtsev

For a complete list of titles visit www.csupoetrycenter.com